RECENT MISTAKES

JAN HORNER

TURNSTONE PRESS

Published with the assistance of the Canada Council
and the Manitoba Arts Council.

Turnstone Press
607-100 Arthur Street
Winnipeg, Manitoba
R3B 1H3

This book was printed by Hignell Printing Limited
for Turnstone Press.

Printed in Canada

Cover illustration: Nicole de Montbrun

Cover design: Robert MacDonald, MediaClones

Some of these poems have previously appeared, or have
been accepted for publication, in *Arts Manitoba, Border
Crossings, CVII, CV2, Dandelion, Dinosaur Review, Poetry
Canada Review*, and *Prairie Fire*.

Canadian Cataloguing in Publication Data

Horner, Jan C. (Jan Cynthia), 1952-

  Recent mistakes

  Poems.
  ISBN 0-88801-125-3

I. Title.

PS8565.O76R4 1988   C811'.54   C88-098032-X
PR9199.3.H67R4 1988

I would like to thank: my sister Kathleen as well as Jane, Jacqui, Donna and Angela for their inspiration and support; Bob Irvine for his letters; Dennis Cooley, Fred Wah and Patrick Friesen for their encouragement and advice; and my editors Pat and David.

Contents

RECENT MISTAKES

"I'm lookin' for something outside of forgiveness."
—Ferron, "Proud crowd/ proud cried"

Cyclist

Every night the bicycle
rides over mountains to me
Every night the man who rides
turns away over the Arctic Circle
He talks slower, softer
but the wheels spin on
I reach up to hold him
he sees only forgotten sheets
on the line
He sees my white picket fence
the sour milk, the dirty laundry
Even my sleeping son
cannot charm the bicyclist

As I dream
blooms at his window
lean out
transmitting desire
Above his bed
the parasol turning
its spokes attempts
to stroke his inner tubes
Picasso blue clown
in a grey kitchen closet
the red enamel windows
signal blood in the bath
As I dream
his fine hair grows on my breasts
thick and black
and dishes in my dark cupboards
glow in frenzy
to iron his shirts

When he comes
the deer will be eating our crabapples
When he comes
the walnut tree will bear fruit
candles will flare up
doors open
and messages will seep
through the walls
And when he comes
my paper bags will hold
cut flowers in water
If it is morning when I wake
my bicycle will be fixed
If it is evening
I will become the bicycle

Each time you leave

Each time you leave
tearing the air away with you
we could say what happens is this:
a woman walks into the ocean
past islands and breakers
and vanishes to our eyes

Her letters float to you slowly
over those sodden expanses
On your shore they become
merely what remains
her dresses that you loved, now discarded
the shells on her bureau that weigh
like so many others
the letters like her hankies
once scented, now musted
the sheets she folded now rotted
and from all the white and yellowed pages
a persistent voice
waves you keep hearing
on the beach all night
long

Going south

you whisper in my ear
so early in the morning
wake me from my sleep and I hear
your smoking over the line and wish
I was the cigarette between your lips
a daily addiction
stirring up blood and neurons
your intimate and potential trouble
your dangerous flirtation
not this woman lying in her chaste bed
her horizontal voice teasing
from heartlands and frozen prairie

I close my eyes
reach my arms around you
my lips around your tongue
I dream us out of this telephone simulation
colliding above Lake Superior
        we are passengers on runaway trains
                you lying between my legs

                we drift south   out of winter

Old growth

If leaves grew out of my head
I'd offer them to you
Would you know at what cost
you'd have my cut stems, odorous sap
forgetting me in this, how hard they were to grow
You see this strangled blooming
as weeds/thorns/brambles
forever slashing never laying down your machete
your rainforest syndrome

I turn to you as to the bowl of flowers
I covet for my piano
like the bust of some magnificent head
Those beautiful blind eyes (a man would say of a woman)
they don't miss their kindness
only their lidded emergency measures
those flirt's eyes that suggest complicity
and portion favour

We are unopened blooms bruised by expectation
how can we survive the frost
let's forget the roses of poets, gardeners
cut off those dead heads, look for new beds
let the melancholy drain out of us
all the way to Hudson Bay
let us believe in fertile ground

I want someone

I want someone to unfold me, shake me out
attend to my creases, brush the hair from my eyes
smooth the furrows in my brow
I want someone to overwhelm me, lay me out
without force or precision
I want someone to subdue that person
who processes and destroys information all night
    (gently and with kisses to my face and hands)
I want someone to chase away those false selves:
sycophants, wimpies, cheats
I want someone to tell me my armies of women
are useless, antiquated
and when the enemy comes over the hill
it will only be one man and he will fall
down at my feet defenceless

Novel lovers

They make superficial notes on small cards
talk into rude telephones examine signatures
Librarians are in the business
of seducing young boys
While explaining the subtleties of the Index
the fallibility of Dr. Johnson
these keepers of books secretly measure youths
for their beds
If they ever succeed
their notion of how such affairs climax
is uninformed and abstract

They send out clandestine love messages
through the catalogues
which never arrive, are never decoded
They do not receive even a little piece of paper
though they desire
billets doux with birds of paradise
pressed between the leaves

Sullenness, sour looks
disguise the migraines and fever
of their life-sickness
Confused by all
they have read
librarians are lost in the maze
in which they imagine themselves
the minotaur
the focus of speculations, fear
passionate research

Such novel lovers
find elegance
in tickertape heroes
J. Alfred Prufrock, Mrs. Dalloway
Cloistered
they escape into a penance
of mundane duties, a life of service
As dust settles on their lashes
something radiates unnoticed
from quartos in their hearts
those books
whose ideas are not questioned
nor ever known

The library dreams

The library dreams of endowment and privilege, of stardom,
a long-running series: the naked stacks, of a life dust-free, a
satellite in space. The library dreams of opening nights,
marble lions, oak shelves, leaded panes, the vital secrets,
happy endings, the weight and meaning, the well-stocked
symmetry. The library dreams of romance, double lives, risks,
rapacious borrowers, unnatural appetites, untimely deaths.
Like an old-fashioned president it dreams of scholarship,
publication, bestsellers, opening books (their collective sigh).
It dreams of drowning photocopy machines in the basement,
in the stinking acidity of their own toner, of laser-printing
those perverts with razors, greasy fingers, fluorescent pens,
metal security strips. The library dreams of health, temperate
zones, of encompassing and holding the world, the universe
of words. Its dreams darken and the library dreams of fire.
This is not a nightmare. It is a lucid dream of release and
return to her underworld and community of souls.

Reference questions

Do you have books auto repair fiction (breasts) time do
books talk get up and walk are salts pink does the earth move I
want the stairs the door, the close encounter sequence of
Uranus
The reference pathfinders, scouts, traffickers in fact
with their confident directions, common sense
They will submerge you with information if you let them
they want you to die satisfied if not happy
The desk where a question on the history of banking
breaks down to linguistic choices
and where to put your money
because Canadian and imperial are contradictory
or the need to locate the author of a dictionary
becomes an accusation of plagiarism
and the advisor's tact the reader's dismay
when a writer much longed for is long dead
and the woman who comes shopping for languages
wanting to be excited by the way words look
or the man beyond tact doing research
on the double life of his father
for whom there are no answers

Does this mean something?
the signs and codes not read or misinterpreted
the world gone astray, out of reach, backlogged, mislabelled or
on a truck bound for the north range
In my library shelves are many parents, brief lives
and if the staff were all propped up dead at their posts
would people still find their way to what they need
would there still be the man like a pig in shit
with his military maps and books-in-print
the woman dying with her distraction of books
dead or alive would the world notice
and does the world exist to become a book?

I guess you read a lot of books . . . ?
the deception of working in a public place
as if you had access to all those books going in and out
those people walking, stopping and asking
by knowing what they read and how they find
as if there weren't a separation of roles
Some would say this is show business;
going live with cataloguing
as if you knew something about a man
because of his forlorn ankle socks
and the woman who may have four daughters
all of them beautiful and at least one dangerous
as if you could tell the man who stands reading
the dictionary so long knows it looks good on him
as if you could make contact through costumes
odd flirtations, shelf codes
as if you could read a book by its cover

Shopping dreams

Maybe she would admit life arrives
unannounced, undressed
She is not framed and captioned:
"What the new woman wears . . . "   or
"I dreamt I conquered Rome in a sarong and stiletto heels"
Despite the accessories, aerodynamic hair
something must survive the hype
How can she tell the boutique actress
when she goes in for her wardrobe rethink
it's all old and ugly
when they are not in the business
of making you beautiful or young
She dreams she is the bitch
who doesn't know how she's unhappy
who goes shopping to find out what she wants
filling her vacuum with manufactured desire
the label and pricetag verifying
other women's work, silent at machines
Of course her dream husband can't get excited
about this but they don't talk business
and have sex once a week
If you look closely
her left shoe is coming off her right foot
her chests are all opening
and she is trembling with hungers
she has barely embraced
and cannot name

What I am doing to change the world

I soothe the digestion of orphans
eat all that's generous
all that's weeping on my plate
I wash my windows
rake leaves
take in laundry
so the Queen will know
Canada is so many houses
clean and mitred in her graces

I think about a mute piano
a tuneless stereo
announce vows of silence
my benefits to raise literacy
in all third worlds
I have my nose fixed
for you tell me this bears
on what develops in Afghanistan
I remember to buy Canadian
pay my taxes
I have written letters to God
talked to strangers
(destroyed the evidence)
I cope with baby kisses
extend my credit

I begin to think like a woman
(start smoking like a man)
I haunt garage sales
presort garbage
and at the very last moment
take in strays

Bluebeard

The way he looks at me
it should be a high school dance
I can see he is an amateur
I threaten him
horror fights fascination
cracking his smooth skin, his brown eyes
I am too new too many tempter woman liar none
of what he knows neither lover nor mother
He suspects I lead a pure life
feeding on royal jelly
books in unknown languages
and windows looking out to sea
He is intrigued by a freak in me
he cannot name and comes back
to examine me for flaws

I walk toward him
a train of light perfecting form
bride of unravished quietness
He misses the obvious forgets himself
Past the rotting crabapples into the forest
he says my pubic hair is Egyptian blue
I tell him his cruelty is kind but it's
the last time he'll see it
that way

Eurydice replies

Only a fragment now
of something we wanted to say
our broken urn
"And I knew these people . . . "
but have lost the thread
and will stand by my words
waiting
though the boat is deep
and water swims round my eyes

I miss you
will now forever
as the world is round and turns
and though my ears lie flat, unperturbed
Our stars are near
and the fish come out
we will waver on our beaches
magnetized
our children crying
our lost blue-veined babies

Leave your cold dinner
write me once more over your table
and hold me under
our legs entwined
like seaweed
your mouth on my neck
a prodigal desire returning
and turning

I see you in deep water
singing, your mouth full of tears
treading a dark undertow
But tell me
while I still remember
while you can touch me
what were you going to say
what were you turning to say

Hawk man

When you left us undefended
I conceived our safety
mine and our son's
rushing upstairs
to snatch him from sleep
and escape out the window
to the trees and flat roof
the clamouring night
its still hawk man
ticking and intense
the sheen of threats
and his expression black
unreadable as the world

Do you remember
I wrote this dream to you
It was only later I understood
you were the man
a coveted, unwanted fate
growing on our house
like a wart
You were the hawk man
winged and oblivious
to the storm around us
the fear and unexpected fascination
growing inside me
a cancer
Only later I admitted
I loved what he represented
like a beautiful suicide
I let it happen

Beauty and the Beast: a revenge tale
(with homage to Jean Cocteau's film)

What Cocteau's film makes clear: the Beast, the prince once released from his spell, and Beauty's false suitor, Avenant, are all played by the same actor and the Beast is more compelling than either handsome rogue or radiant prince. Avenant, who follows Beauty to the chateau to steal the Beast's jewels, dies when a statue of Diana on the enchanted grounds shoots him with an arrow. Avenant's face contorts in pain just as Beauty tells the Beast she loves him and he is freed from his spell. Beauty and the new prince, Ardent, float upwards, magically transported to his kingdom.

I

The summer I was nineteen practising
pirouettes, fouetté turns—as close
to perfection as I would ever come
Ten years later you gave up
exiting downstage
and in all decency
why couldn't you wait
I will turn cool and elegant
but with disquieting slowness
like animated stone

The ships, our parents' hopes for us
set out launching our fortunes
and on our birthday
capsize, go aground
Casting misery to the sea
I dive naked recovering pearls
our blind and useless eyes
and like the sea
I have something to say
churning it over and over

Why do roses matter?
when the real problem
was your desire to steal Beauty
(there are no princes)
and your need for me to play Beast
If you wanted wildness
why the control and distance
impenetrable front
I was supposed to save you
from some crone's enchantment
This is a fairy tale I am forced to break

II

I will haunt your best love scenes
coming through the walls
like a flower unfurling
sonic petals
I will stick out my tongue
from the mantle
and roll my eyes
with the candlesticks
I will be yawning
with the napkins
I will be there at the climax

Be watchful as the statue turns
and my arrow flies piercing you the false lover
so your gilded, romantic form can float
out of enchantment, home
your nuptial flight with the beauty
who will soon mourn
"Where is my beast?"

Walking on air

Sometimes
I can walk on air
To the dreamer suspended in sleep
not such a blue moon feat
I merely rise
while something in the body lets go
lifting off
as if it was all in the shoulders
Like a growing up
a pod of new bones
opening to elevate the spine
and the lower limbs
cumbrous and heavy-muscled
melting into cones

But it happens always
in rooms with doors and hallways
Doors with high sills
I am upside down
walking on my head
talking with my toes
This explains the speechlessness
the spaces ghost white
distractions pulled
to some other gravity

Whose dream is this
An old house, the grandfather's
a house underwater
deserted, unwelcoming
I do not enter but am there
agile, moving
in reversed direction

Picture of "Bill at Niagara Falls, 1948"

It is the spooky or spooked eyes
distrustful, fighting their own fairness
not a beautiful suit but the lithe, thoughtless body
great shoulders, strong jaw
the mouth unfriendly, even cruel
you look out resolute standing up for the record
but uncomfortable, a fear of heights, the falls at your back
Two men in fact, both poised for action
pretending they are ready to leap the wrought iron
Did you think: behind the camera is my father the old
  horsetrader
waiting for news of his own manhood second-hand
On the back you wrote as if to efface yourself:
"the fellow is Boyd Douglas from UBC" (I am invisible)
Someone wrote on the front later: "Bill at Niagara Falls"

Though you still dream of wild animals
animals chasing a small boy animal
great smelly brutish and sexual
If you had ever allowed the question
could you have said what scared you
where you came from my tall mute father
with fair eyelashes and brows blue true blue eyes
(the better to squint with)
my father who would have been a great farmer but no cowboy
who could have learned many secrets about weather and soil
who always wanted to invest in commodities
who went east to work in American goods
underground installations, mines and turbines
Canada's mineral resources rocky shield
a boy from the land in the west: silent without grief
but this need to deny your father's kingdom
what has driven you, what drives you away nightly

If we were allowed different voices, I'd say:
You have never asked me for anything
and know I can't save you
Kiss me just this once, I have your photo and
my getaway car is waiting

My mother is sculpting me

I

My mother looks at me (all my life) she recognizes her
maiden aunts the way my head inclines does not need to
look   sees my posture the first persistent   smile uneven
and secret "your colour is good" she says "have you lost
weight" "my beautiful daughter" she says she watches my
progress reputation the men   saw me take my first step
and   my mind's eye wonders what held/holds me   poised
on the brink of escape   looking into my dissatisfaction
she   offers food scrutinizes my books my children for signs
of change she sees how I am like my father face and fortune
but what my father was never allowed the fright, panic and
yearning "don't screw up your face" I please her she has
dressed me I continue to look at her Vogue patterns and she
smiles when I am that smart woman in her smart dresses her
concise correct gestures speech

II

My mother touches me (all my life): cleaning, powdering,
spanking, fitting, brushing, wiping, clipping, cutting common
gestures of care   &   those sibilant caresses honeybun her
sweetie pie her lap a chair for my plump flesh she explored
my small ears thick hair her manicured hands the thin gold
band now her lapis rings her soft skin holding my wrist her
examining my freckled back her hands in my hair all hands
her hand taking my arm the sudden idea of my sturdiness
and support   the surprise in our conversation

III

My mother is sculpting me from notions she has formed (all
my life) using her pink plasticene and when that runs out
filling the cranium with turquoise and lime (my vast and
lurid brains) she takes light to my skin the hollows and planes
finding what is flat after so many years of looking turning me
round measuring what she has missed   touching small
curves feeling unseen mechanics   amazed at what I've
become what she's made what I've made and me not
recognizing me seeing I'm not yet finished   something is
still unfleshed   I know without being able to tell her   I will
continue the portrait emerging from time to time   pink,
lurid, alive   in all my glowing substance

A Vancouver story

We walk down the hill
I ran up three years ago
athletic breathless and led
The same hill now
absorbed by midnight
a moonlit midsummer
we walk past lawns cut for gnomes
and public splendour
and see ourselves
in the enfolding cleft of mountains
the giant trees framing
the unimaginable bowel of sea
and away into its city
neon tower turrets
the brilliant fortress
buttressed with light
Princesses
we speak of various enchantments
we have witnessed in our bodies
to keep us snow white
we speak of our taboos and secrets
and at this turn walking into queenhood
we try out our murky translations
our talking ourselves
into and out of night

WHAT NOT TO PUT IN A LETTER

"My letter is a paper hoop.
   when I break through it, you will be imprisoned."
                —Robert Lowell after Engenio Montale
                   "News from Mount Amiata" (*Imitations*)

Valentine

Why don't you start by telling me
how bea-u-tiful I am
how my 77 moving parts excite you
how delightful that I have
two arms, two legs, a nose
Show me your spangled imaginations
give me some sign of your dangerous life

Forget about your receding hairline
and the distance between us
my bed is small and low
Forget your cigarettes
My lips will blow smoke rings for you
I can wash your hair with my feet

Ask me about my dog, my freckles
keep me talking I will warm up
I have chairs inside me for you
where is your couch
We can open windows, make beds
What's in your heartbox
give me those mild pangs
I will swallow them whole

Touch me with your hands
I will bend
Kiss me on the neck
I will turn and open
This is your last chance
why don't you start

Opening your letter

Opening your letter
I find feathers from a bird
I am not allowed to touch
the map of a place
I will never visit
an ad in Hindi
for a movie I will not see
Is it true for words
that it no longer matters
what they say
only
that they are sent
mysterious forms
silent images
released from any vow
of relevance
or communication

Closing your letter
I turn from a window
that always
distracts me from you
Which of us is more convincing
now that we know
each other's reflection
I cut and send my hands
but they unclasp
before you
despite our care
in packing, unwrapping
What did we ever have
to celebrate us
but selective memory
our big-screen projection

Letter from a buffalo girl

Lick me cowboy
across the wide open ranges
across the still night air
that feeds your horse races and cowboy hopes
Come down off that big horse with its slobbery kisses
see how the fire reddens my hands
and dries my eyes
how I must wait in this fenced corral
for you to come home with your lasso tricks
your stories, your ribbons gone ragged
and you smelling like wildflowers and sage
What holds me to this purpose so absent
my garden, the cows, the washing, the accounts
the company now rare
so many chances gone over the horizon into the sunset
I wonder what a new place could mean
a new place not so big and blue and noble
not so empty of faces and time
where the wind doesn't bully
the trees know their places and dogs don't go wild
I'm not bound by your big hands
dwarfed by your Stetson
You should see how much I carry
more than a campfire tune:
"your sweet and shiny eyes
are like the stars above Laredo"
This time I'll be the one to go free.

Gretel's letter

I'm lost in the woods
found a temporary cottage
but I'm lost in the woods
with my brother unwell
working through the strange dreams
the lost causes of our first griefs
the private reckonings and unmarked graves
and what enchantment
made me lose my nerve so young
and what will go next
my voice once pliant and charged

In the darkness of this place
so light on the surface
like Switzerland its barely concealed depressions
this resort where whole cities
confront their secret and wrongheaded desires
My brother trails a slow leak
a thin line of sawdust marks his path
Together we are twin seals
complacent and sexless
tweedledumb   tweedledee
We ignore the holes
all our sweet holdings on, the polite words
and gentle tugs
we want to stay near the sand forever
beached seals unchanged, growing old
with all the sweet cakes and cream
our land of hearts desire.

Writing you

Writing you, the longing for it
the fear and flood of it, the wrong words
I go on believing this over and over
we are in a great soft bed of paper
we are alone together for the first time
and my hands go on working across and down
I echo your disbelief and abandon
In the best parts we dance
our tango fuelled by tender juices
but I hit you, no accident you devour me
I build us up again, you disintegrate
I am a twice-beheaded monster, you a mirage
We are stuck somewhere in the hips, the buttocks
unconnected at our heads, our hands without lips
but your awkward hands so strong around me
and the one seductive whisper
as your message falls out of the envelope
(I will sniff around its lips for your tongue)
the words rushing on without us
in my head never deciding, never having to
about my address, the right dress, my undress, my indirection
Everything recedes, descends, comes down to
fragments secret and fragile
your double kisses, my carefully chosen stamps
Maybe I am in love
with the postman his punctuality
his full bag
his suitor's diffidence

Junk mail

Joyce dear female logic breaks too many
hearts both sides of the snow fence our
tired and involute stroll your vulvular
demand I refuse linear volvo functions
goal maintenance but I'm no family
man despite so much paper on this desk
typing errors unanswered bills errors of
imagination slings arrows ideas you fire
this way could make a difference if only
our odorous disco-magnificence could hold
temporary the foul-mouthed light brigade
the reality break-in (imagine a situation
worsening at a more clipped rate)   you
become so political put in your own
sparks change your own oil I have wanted
a displaced mind too long now   trapped
with no desire to exit diseased and
irresponsible I have nice teeth your
sweat like orchid tears reminds me
I owe you the confession we all refuse
to make please let me come home to your
white kitchen   don't bitchchch hon- neeey

Night run

I run out to the night
because it is convenient and lonely
But the time surprises me
Trees rush everywhere
their crash and heavings warn
of green storms at sea
Sheet lightning wars on the horizon
Skunk trails, manure and blooms
pump messages into my blood
Pedestrians mutate in the fluorescence
headlights menace me
I know the paranoia stirred up
in these shadows
And the wind comes with me
behind and beside pushing and pulled

Porch lights of houses
wink in domestic safety
There is a man inside
reading
His house is lit for comfort
and cooking, sweet childhoods
and summer warmth

I must find my house
swaying and embraced by elms
There is no fireplace
but a light waiting for me
it has no companion
shining above my desk
Soon I will sit down before it
words running onto a page
soon I will write myself and you

Postage inland: letter home

I am writing myself
into a convincing fiction
My letters take on the charm
of unreliable narrators
You can discern an evolution
the smoothness of whipped eggs
Will there be climax denouement
a central action or icon
Or have I entered
territories of unmeaning
Writing not to charge or keep you
but to let words
find and break you

When I dreamt her
what was she doing in that glorious place
by the river, the autumn twilight
What frightened her, whose dark voice
her manuscript
crisp and luminous
wrapped about her, a well-cut toga
I remember we came over like thugs
attracted to her indecent exposure
Won't someone please advise me
this has gone on too long

Letter to an art lover

"Emotional cripples don't believe the tree moves in the mind.
They believe their mind moves because the tree is unjust."
—David Donnell

My dress opens, an umbrella
as we go downstairs
and you, a series of shuttered rooms
with hidden cameras
record soundlessly:
how the flaring bell rings
our deafening silence
Flickering children's faces
birds your hands describe and follow
I feel them flutter some extra chamber
that beats about the heart
The world and its acid frames constantly burn you
At night you put
dark glasses on

Under the city's dark canopy
you construe meaning
from industrial turquoise and rust
you bless insulation pink
You claim to have wrestled
with the life of machines
Your statistics and 5 dollars max.
are attempts to pretend
your interests are merely functional
but I listen and
Segovialike
you pluck inventions

You say a tree moves in the wind
does not change when you look at it
as a child does or a woman
I have been the tree whose chlorophyll senses
energy and vegetable love
You are not wooden only struck open
like an umbrella
yourself a rooted wonder, a question
In my last letter I will whisper
(do you hear me?)
trees have always asked us to be different
there is no still life

Lithium letter

I want to know what you are doing
so you told me
you have the neap and lunar tides
fixed to your bicycle
and the salmon are dying
as they do every year

Language flowed together
in and out, in and out of us
but we left the documents and letters
our common notion of shelter
and collapsed without warning
not for us the festering and self hatred
months on end

I will be in Winnipeg
for years
waiting for the coast to clear
riding out my maturity and irradiation
Your sentiments do not travel
and my festival is filled
with absence

How can we prepare for the unspeakable
we might as well sit down
in our deck chairs and wait

Dead letter

This is a letter I cannot send
Passing through so many hands and mechanical claws
suggestion flakes, combustion sputters
affection lies, curdles, calculates interest
In your hands
the words might slide off the page
and fly like cinders
into your dead eye

What will I do with my dead letter
I will bury it
I will plant it
Its fast and supple roots
will push up around your house
invade your windows
thrusting its blooms and their scent
into your cryptic face
stinging you with their pistils
their shadows
impinging on your grief and despair
whispering:
try remorse

Inside you
there is already an envelope
with an egg white seal
and it's addressed to nobody
all those it may concern

Postcard #1: Montreal, after he left

Here we are!
I am not in the picture
was absent when it was taken
having just finished
sitting in a laundromat
quietly tearing our house down
So good to know a plumber finally
The lady at the kiosk must write
she says nothing that isn't prepared and sweet

I intend to reply better more later
details will sort themselves further regards
I may have included a kiss
but cannot say for sure
my shoes starched the way they are
Do you still collect toy robots
nice mementoes of solid state
I have forsworn mechanical means
of transport
Your conversation suffers
from the ambiguity of brief cards
Must run on my arms with my legs love all—write pages
XOX-OX-OX

Postcard #3: Canadian shield, the way to be tough

You would love this place
the life spent in musk oil
What shuffles through your drawers
and pages or why haven't you written
as if one night in Wawa
could fill up   all those years
and we had all the seconds promised in our watches

Sean misses his dark father
and is learning to play hockey
en français
Come down to tea
and I'll put you with the daisies
You can admire
the sword and pink gun
Sean says I carry
and we'll see who gets to pour

Can you find a mailbox—red, proximal, efficient
or at least a letter carrier
They read diagonally
                and for speed
                      but
they may crack the code
before   we do

Postcard #4: New York, a pomegranate

This place so ripe and red
and doing all the wrong things
New Year's Day went jogging
around the reservoir early Central Park
with all the empty bottles and its sad sun
Picked up a doctor over lunch
an anaesthetist
who spoke Polish and wanted me
or what I knew about Magritte

In this place so ripe and red
and doing all the wrong things
my insides break open
so many jewelled seeds: a pomegranate
the juices seeping down to stain purple
the delicate organs below
why must I fly half a continent
to awaken yearnings delicate, jewelled
how can we be content
to feast on rotten apples, our sour regret

Postcard #5: Vancouver, the retreat

I am in an attic
reading and writing
an airplane overhead
wrapped in the traffic of distant radios
children crying
the sight of leviathan-ships passing

Rachael and I went swimming
she said
you were counselling the dead
out of sight out of mind
I said
I bought French bread
for breakfast, missing
what I cannot help will not change
do not forget
Too bad I fell between what you wanted
and what you net
Aggrieved by my luck, your gift to me
we are capable of everything
and make nothing but paper work
write soon—or remain unread

Postcard #7: Winnipeg, the best revenge

Since hearing no further
I went dancing
with any faithless man
My soul comes and goes
profligate, bruised blue
with music it blows red and gold
for company
the lacewing players delicate and starred
with such high temptations
we feel the rain shower and bow
clouds prickle our toes
and the falling and turning
shoes tapping patent and pulsing
my mouth wide calls to angels
sound waves which carry horses
their combs on my mane
I'm off with stars in my ears
dragonflies stirring on my dress
rustling in the net of my legs
catch me catch me catch

African letters

I write from the subtropics
"the ocean is so warm
—you can't imagine—
like swimming in tea"
are you still cycling
in wool legwarmers
your fingers going numb with cold
After the ocean
we come home to rats in the pantry
dog packs attacking a bushbuck
no petrol and this morning
an earth tremor

Africa, all her prodigies
are within us
belittling your telegram
infringing on our letters and private griefs
Civil strife is looming
in this tribal country
The dissidents will not be allowed to leave
though I pack and unpack my bags
over and over
Kidnappings and violence
snipe on
and mortar shells I see across the border
are also in this bedroom
Marriages are falling apart around us
our letters fall open
hysterical

Letter to her son

This morning I miss you
because there are little boys here
all the way from Nigeria
two of them, only one of you
their distance a reminder of our separation
I have no bail bonds and no excuses

We went down to the river
the boys caught no fish with their worms
despite their dancing, their lilting voices
they wanted me to catch their hard pitches
they too want their father's praise and muscles
but will take my admiration between their white teeth
Because they are video sportsmen
they think Winnipeg is a city of blue bombs
as if they knew your star wars
as if boys the world over did not love soldiers
Wanting to win all arguments
they ask why Canadians are so crazy
Will you be quick enough for Nick and Oko
all the third world contenders?

The cat here had kittens
while we were talking on the bed
before angelus rang through the window
The cat here had kittens and it's your birthday
your cake will have nine candles
I am always falling over you, your shoes
your nine neat lives with their cats and kittens

I'm thinking about making a cake
the kind with pennies and wishes
a cake big enough to feed birds
with enough crumbs to take you through the mazes
of all those who plot against you
never any lighter or sweeter
so swallow your cares and eat my cake

And as you blow out the candles
here are my wishes:
that you always have room for another
that you always write
and keep off the booze and candies
and forget the ready formulas for pleasing all
that you dream us out of your warheads
that you can tell a good woman from a hopeless one
and keep a light burning always
that you will be the one man to leave me
unscathed

A letter to my mother

So this is my life
looking away to the trees
the rocket spires
now milked and cleansed
by the baby no longer inside
but whose drama I am now into
my little boy with his rights
and perfect teeth

Having left my son
I come to the coast to write another
to write as a mother
to remember your father
writing, a guest life
inviting my own retirement
Morning wakes us to different excuses
flowers in the rooms
Writing, a terrible work if you can get it
all my versions gone
over the hill and home

The fear of my being alone
comforts us with truth
if we leave it long enough
if we leave it last and later
Mr. Wrong will become your father
You will understand his slippers
the old man shirts
the tea towel round his waist
as the reason your daughter still smokes
And that this is where
I've always been headed
to someone's son
your father, my lover
a woman worth her weight
in desire
you should know
your loving child
you, her first lover, her first speaker
she will have courage
and will find once more
all those who cherish her
truly

Sister letters

I

Who would buy such a thing
our father says of the giant spider
you send my son
He would be surprised
the lines we buy from men
the stories he sold to us

You wonder
that time at Stratford
we saw The Tempest
but do you remember the island
its strong willed father

and her classic choice: Wildman or exotic prince

when did we lose
        our sense of moment
how did we allow
        those raw Ferdinands to enter
and become our new brave worlds

                and you write: *I noticed his shoes in particular*
                                  nice leather Italian black loafers
                                  not so appealing no longer wistful

and why didn't they learn their parts
and know when to speak
        O you wonder   Miranda!
you wonder

II

later you write: *Sarah joined us at lunch. She is a*
bitch of course but bright and
witty. It's always nice to talk to
people when they are at ease.

I don't understand
your games of resistance your subtle decencies
the scorn of your nostrils
we wanted so much or
all you have spent and wasted
to deny life insurance, washing machines

What can we untangle
preserve as narrative logic
What do your artefacts tell us
about how far we've come
And why are you with
those awful people
the boys unhappy who can no longer seduce
their mothers

You are a comet
pursuing conversation
restless meaning

III

For my birthday you write: *I am like this kangaroo*
                                with undeveloped arms
                                and huge feet
                                more our father's child
                                than I care to admit

at night our father lies between us
the sleeping giant
you whisper: *touch him*
                                everyone does everyone must
But I see more
than your sculpted Egyptian head
Montreal fag hag with Gitanes
and talk of tight cunt

        You never have

Have we made this unhappy woman
between us
out of postage and letters
your anger, my grief
        a woman self-exiled
        her frontier urban, blinkered
        at the limits of response

Who would guess
our afternoon ballet classes
would become dayglo boots
tulle tutus at the end of civilization
canned, on film
in your empty fridge

IV

        you write: *It's like wearing odd socks. You*
                                 come to prefer it after awhile.

We exchange our dreams and stories
imagine the worst for each other
You will become old and scattered
like the clothes you affect
as wonderfully repellent
as the iridescent lizard you carry
in your transparent bag

      While you tell me this
      did I ever
go to a window and cry
to those compatriots who would listen
      Canada my husband is an idiot

V

Will we continue to pass on tall authority
choosing men for physical comfort
a familiar message of deep trouble
treasure sublime but circumspect
            Our remittance men
            coming as if by lottery
            with no chances to win
Daddy
            why didn't the story go
we threw them in the river
then, happy sisters, went home

Let's apply our lipstick carefully
and think in all seriousness
about what we will swallow
for how little we need
to be happy, after all

            what we always wanted
            is in the sunroom
            of our grandfather's house